grill pan cookbook

great recipes for stovetop grilling

Jamée Ruth

Photographs by David Roth

CHRONICLE BOOKS
SAN FRANCISCO

This Chronicle Books LLC edition published in 2006.

ISBN: 0-8118-5352-7

The Library of Congress has cataloged the previous edition
as follows:

Ruth, Jamée.
    The grill pan cookbook: great recipes for stovetop
grilling/by Jamée Ruth; photographs by David Roth.
        p.   cm.
    Includes index.
    ISBN 0-8118-2417-9 (pbk.)
    1. Barbecue cookery.   2. Grill pans.   I. Title.
TX840.B3R88 1999   98-48789
641.5'784—dc21   CIP

Manufactured in China

Designed by Stuart McKee
Prop styling by Robin Turk
Food styling by Janet Miller
    and Christine Anthony-Masterson

Distributed in Canada by
Raincoast Books
9050 Shaughnessy Street
Vancouver, British Columbia V6P 6E5

10 9 8 7 6 5 4 3 2 1

Chronicle Books LLC
85 Second Street
San Francisco, California 94105

www.chroniclebooks.com

TABLE OF CONTENTS

Vegetables

Seafood

Meats

ACKNOWLEDGMENTS

One of my goals in life has always been to be loyal to those who give me strength, for ours is an exchange of energy.

My gratitude goes to an extraordinary spirit full of enthusiasm, my personal assistant Lindsey Etheridge, who always kept her eyes on the road and her hands on the wheel for both of us. Thank you, Bill LeBlond, for spotting me from across the room. The team at Chronicle Books, what a pleasure to work with such extraordinary talent. Brigit Binns, thank you for keeping me within the guidelines. Laura Reiley, my escort to writing in "house style." For making everything in this book look good enough to eat, I thank photographer David Roth, food stylist Janet Miller, food stylist Christine Anthony-Masterson, and for her extra attention and time, a special thank you to the very talented prop stylist, Robin Turk.

Thank you to the following companies for their continued support and contributions for the recipe testing and photography of this book: All-Clad Metalcrafters; Wusthof-Trident of America, Inc.; Morton and Bassett Spices; House of Smoke, Inc.; Bloomingdale's; Sur la Table; Calphalon Corporation; Le Creuset of America; Lodge Manufacturing Company; Black and Decker; and KitchenAid.

INTRODUCTION

I have always been attracted to people who know more than I do. Never intimidated by them, I recognize the opportunity to learn something new. My career has required that I experiment with the unfamiliar and explore new culinary methods. Through my travels as a private chef, I have found it is best to observe the local people. I have watched them at markets, curious to know what they were buying and what tools they intended to use in preparation. (I can remember shocking a few citizens by pointing at an unfamiliar item and inquiring with my usual enthusiasm about its purpose.) I have seen the most peculiar devices create spectacular culinary magic, and cooking techniques that remain unknown except to those who have passed them down from generation to generation. When I discovered the grill pan, I immediately recognized a unique style of cooking that would inevitably change my life. I had finally found a cooking method that enhances flavor without diminishing the integrity of the food.

I now present to you a culinary revolution. Before you play with fire over the barbecue, consider the option of a grill pan. Surrender no more to the seasons of the sun, for you can enjoy delicious food, cooked to absolute perfection, any night that you wish to stay inside.

With recipes ranging from Lobster Tails with Roasted Garlic to Cowboy Porterhouse Steak, Asparagus with Orange Essence to Smoked Duck Sausage with Red Pear Sauce, you will enjoy new and familiar dishes while learning the art of this exciting approach to naturally healthy cooking. This book will enable you to prepare a meal that will start a controversy . . . all in one pan. Allow me to welcome you to a brave new world of grilling.

One part cookbook, one part technical manual, the *Grill Pan Cookbook* is your guide to limitless success with a new piece of cooking equipment. Once you have mastered this method of cooking with the recipes in this book, you will be inspired to add a contemporary flair to your own favorite dishes.

Several grill pans are on the market these days, but I encourage you to try one with a non-stick finish. It will afford you the luxury of cooking without adding oil to your pan. The single most important key to success in your adventure with this new way of cooking is that you must preheat your grill pan over medium heat until very hot. By doing this you create an evenly heated cooking surface ready for grilling. Would you put food on a cold barbecue?

Tips, Tricks, and Techniques

The purpose of this chapter is to explain the essentials that will enable your grill pan to perform at its maximum potential. The grill pan is not just another pan, it is a new cooking technique. Whether you are a novice or an experienced grill pan user, it is important that you read this chapter before proceeding.

Cleaning

The most effective cleaning tool for a grill pan is a hard nylon scrubber, which allows you to reach between the ridges.

Food Temperature

The first thing I do when I walk into my kitchen is remove the food to be prepared from the refrigerator. You will get the best results from your grill pan if you allow food to warm to room temperature. This is especially important with meats, seafood, and poultry so they will cook evenly all the way through.

Preheat Your Grill Pan

It is a common misconception that a high flame will somehow speed up or improve your cooking. High heat will damage your grill pan, period. It is imperative that you preheat your grill pan over *medium* heat until very hot. To do this, turn your stove on medium, place the pan on the burner, and leave it completely undisturbed for at least 5 minutes. This will create a perfectly even grilling surface within your pan.

Seasoning Food

Because cooking in the grill pan seals in the natural juices of all foods, excessive seasoning is not necessary. In most cases, salt and freshly ground pepper is all that you will need to use. I prefer to use kosher salt. Available at most grocery stores, kosher salt is free of additives and has a coarser texture than ordinary table salt. However, table salt may be substituted in equal amounts in any of the recipes. Any oil that is called for in the following recipes is brushed onto the foods before you grill them. Light olive oil, which is filtered after it is pressed, is specified in many of my recipes because it has a lighter color, scent, and taste than virgin or extra-virgin olive oil. It also has a higher smoking point, which makes it perfect for cooking at higher heats. Never pour oil into a grill pan.

Serving Sizes

Most recipes in this book are for two or four people. This is important in order to avoid overcrowding the grill pan. Moist foods produce so much liquid that they will poach instead of grill. Also, if cooking for two, the meat and vegetables can be cooked in the same pan.

Turning Meats, Fish, and Poultry

You should never have to turn meats, fish, and poultry more than once. When the flesh is ready to be turned it will lift off the pan easily.

Warm Plates

The second thing I do when I walk into the kitchen is place the plates in a warm oven. The basic principle is cold food on cold plates, hot food on warm plates. To heat your plates, put them in the oven at 150 degrees and do not remove them until you are ready to serve.

Utensils

Tongs are the basic utensil for success when cooking in a grill pan, because they allow you to maneuver the food around your pan without piercing it and releasing the juices. If your grill pan has a non-stick finish, I recommend using plastic or wood utensils.

Vegetables

I suppose it was asparagus that gave me my first grill pan epiphany. A brush
of olive oil, a little salt and pepper, and I knew I was experiencing this vegetable the
way it was intended. In an instant, steamed asparagus seemed waterlogged
and flavorless. I had finally discovered how to have hot, sweet, crunchy vegetables
in minutes. Bell peppers, eggplant, and those little jewels, baby artichokes—
they were all perfect, effortlessly surrendering their natural sugars. Imagine . . .
your mouth watering for vegetables!

IT'S A WARM SUMMER DAY, AND I FIND MYSELF CONTEMPLATING DINNER AT TWO IN THE AFTERNOON. I HAVE JUST MADE A PITCHER OF FRESH LEMONADE AND SAT DOWN WITH A POUND OF UNSHELLED PEAS. AFTER TWO GLASSES OF LEMONADE I PEER DOWN AT THE FRUIT OF MY LABOR: ONE FULL CUP OF FRESH-SHELLED SUMMER PEAS. WHEN YOU TASTE THE FRESH BITE OF SUMMER WITH SWEET, TINY PEARL ONIONS, I AM SURE YOU WILL AGREE THAT THIS DISH IS WELL WORTH THE TIME. TRY IT AS A SIDE TO THE COWBOY PORTERHOUSE STEAK WITH GREEN PEPPERCORN SAUCE (PAGE 72).

Pearl Onions and Sweet Peas

SERVES 2 AS A SIDE DISH

1 cup fresh, shelled sweet peas

1 cup peeled pearl onions

1 tablespoon light olive oil

$1/4$ teaspoon salt

$1/4$ teaspoon freshly ground pepper

In a medium glass or nonreactive metal bowl, gently toss together the peas, onions, olive oil, salt, and pepper.

Preheat a grill pan over medium heat until very hot. Add the peas and onions to the grill pan and cook for 5 minutes, tossing frequently. Serve immediately.

THE OLIVE OIL FROM THE ROASTED GARLIC (PAGE 29) IS THE
PERFECT BASTING SAUCE FOR THIS RECIPE. USE CAUTION
WHEN SLICING THE STEAMED ARTICHOKES. THEY ARE VERY DELICATE
AND MAY FALL APART EASILY.

Grilled Artichokes

SERVES 2 AS A SIDE DISH

2 medium artichokes

1 medium lemon, halved

$1/4$ cup light olive oil

$1/4$ teaspoon salt

$1/4$ teaspoon freshly ground pepper

To prepare the artichokes, trim off the thorny tips of the outer leaves with small scissors. As you work, rub the cut parts of the artichokes with lemon to prevent discoloration. Slice the stem off to form a flat bottom. Set the artichokes, stem side down, in a steamer basket within a pan containing 2 to 3 inches of boiling water. Cover and steam until bases are tender, about 30 minutes. Cool slightly and, when cool enough to handle, gently cut the artichokes in half lengthwise. Assemble the artichokes cut side up on a platter or cutting board. Brush the cut sides with olive oil and season with salt and pepper.

Preheat a grill pan over medium heat until very hot. Place the artichokes in the pan cut side down and cook for 10 minutes. Brush the tops of the artichokes with olive oil and season with salt and pepper. Turn and cook for 5 minutes more. Turn again and cook cut side down for a minute, just to heat through. Transfer the artichokes to a warm plate and serve.

THIS IS MY FAVORITE SALAD TO HAVE AFTER STEAK. THE
KEY TO THIS RECIPE IS FINDING GOOD TOMATOES. ALTHOUGH
BEEFSTEAK TOMATOES ARE FEATURED, IF YOU CAN GET
YOUR HANDS ON SOME BEAUTIFUL HEIRLOOM TOMATOES—
BY ALL MEANS USE THEM!

Beefsteak Tomato – Red Onion Salad

SERVES 2 AS A SALAD

1 large beefsteak tomato, cored
and cut into $1/_4$-inch slices

1 medium red onion, cut into
$1/_4$-inch slices

$1/_4$ cup light olive oil

$1/_4$ teaspoon salt

$1/_4$ teaspoon freshly ground pepper

1 head of romaine lettuce,
washed, dried, trimmed, and
halved lengthwise

$1/_2$ cup crumbled blue cheese

Preheat a grill pan over medium heat
until very hot. With a pastry brush, lightly
coat the tomato and red onion slices with
olive oil and season with salt and pepper.
Add to the pan and cook 4 minutes on
each side. Place lettuce halves on plates.
Top each with grilled tomatoes and onions
and sprinkle with the cheese.

THIS IS ONE OF MY FAVORITE VEGETABLE RECIPES BECAUSE
THE ASPARAGUS GETS A SMOKY FLAVOR DURING THE
GRILLING PROCESS. I RECOMMEND JUMBO ASPARAGUS OR THE
LARGEST YOU CAN FIND, AS THE THINNER ASPARAGUS
WILL WILT DOWN TO NOTHING. TAKE THE TIME TO PEEL THE
BOTTOM TWO INCHES OF THE ASPARAGUS STALKS; IT IS
WELL WORTH THE EFFORT.

Asparagus with Orange Essence and Almonds

SERVES 2 AS A SIDE DISH

1 pound jumbo asparagus

1 tablespoon light olive oil

$1/4$ teaspoon salt

$1/4$ teaspoon freshly ground pepper

1 tablespoon orange zest

1 tablespoon ground almonds

Snap off the ends of the asparagus by gently bending each stalk. Soak the stalks in cold water for 15 minutes to loosen any dirt and refresh them. Peel the bottom 2 inches of the stalks with a sharp vegetable peeler. Pat dry and place on a cutting board.

Preheat a grill pan over medium heat until very hot. Brush the asparagus with olive oil and season with salt and pepper. Add to the pan and cook for 7 minutes, shaking the pan frequently to rotate the spears. Sprinkle the orange zest over the top and cook for an additional 2 minutes, continuing to shake the pan. Transfer to warm plates, sprinkle the ground almonds over the top, and serve immediately.

THIS COULD BE CALLED THE "KISSING COUSINS SALAD" BECAUSE RADICCHIO AND ENDIVE ARE CLOSELY RELATED COUSINS FROM THE CICHORIUM FAMILY. BELGIAN ENDIVE IS A SMALL, WHITE AND LIGHT GREEN COLORED, CIGAR-SHAPED HEAD OF TIGHTLY PACKED LEAVES. RADICCHIO DI VERONA IS A SMALL, LOOSE HEAD OF BURGUNDY RED LEAVES. BOTH ARE AVAILABLE AT MOST SUPERMARKETS.

Grilled Radicchio and Endive Salad

SERVES 2 AS A SALAD OR 4 AS A SIDE DISH

1 head of radicchio, core trimmed, halved lengthwise

1 head of Belgian endive, core end trimmed slightly, halved lengthwise

2 tablespoons light olive oil

1 teaspoon dried thyme, crumbled

$1/4$ teaspoon salt

$1/2$ teaspoon freshly ground pepper

$1/2$ teaspoon balsamic vinegar

Preheat a grill pan over medium heat until very hot. With a pastry brush, lightly coat the cut sides of the radicchio and endive with olive oil and season with thyme, salt, and pepper. Grill the vegetables cut side down for 5 minutes. Brush the rounded tops with a little more olive oil and season as above. Turn the vegetables and grill for 2 minutes more. Drizzle with vinegar and serve immediately.

COMMONLY FOUND IN STIR-FRIES, THESE VEGETABLES
MAINTAIN THEIR ELEGANT APPEARANCE WHEN GENTLY COOKED
IN A GRILL PAN. BASTE THE VEGETABLES LIBERALLY
WITH THE SAUCE WHILE THEY ARE COOKING TO SEASON THEM
THOROUGHLY. I PREFER LOW-SODIUM SOY SAUCE, WHICH
HAS A MELLOWER FLAVOR, ALTHOUGH YOU CAN SUBSTITUTE
EQUAL AMOUNTS OF REGULAR SOY SAUCE.

Baby Bok Choy with Sweet Baby Corn and Water Chestnuts

SERVES 2 AS A SIDE DISH

BASTING SAUCE

1 tablespoon low-sodium
  soy sauce

2 teaspoons grated fresh ginger

1 teaspoon rice vinegar

2 tablespoons light olive oil

---

4 heads baby bok choy,
  halved lengthwise

1 15-ounce can baby corn,
  well drained

2 8-ounce cans whole water
  chestnuts, well drained

To make the basting sauce:
Combine the soy sauce, ginger, vinegar, and oil in a small glass or nonreactive metal bowl and set aside.

Place the bok choy, corn, and water chestnuts on a platter and brush them generously with the basting sauce.

Preheat a grill pan over medium heat until very hot. Grill the vegetables for about 5 minutes, basting often. Turn the vegetables and cook an additional 5 minutes, basting often. Transfer to warm plates and serve immediately.

WHEN YOU HAVE COMPANY AND THE BARBECUE BUFFS ARE
OUTSIDE PLAYING OVER THE COALS, YOUR GRILL PAN SHOULD BE
HARD AT WORK INSIDE WITH THIS IDEAL ACCOMPANIMENT.
THIS DISH IS A PERFECT MAIN COURSE OR A COLORFUL SIDE
DISH TO MEAT, FISH, OR CHICKEN.

Summer Vegetables with Cherry Tomato Salsa

SERVES 2 AS A MAIN COURSE OR 4 AS A SIDE DISH

4   medium pattypan squash, halved

4   baby zucchini, halved lengthwise

1   cup cipolline or pearl onions,
     peeled

1   medium red bell pepper,
     cored, seeded, and sliced into
     $1/4$-inch strips

2   medium carrots, peeled and
     sliced into $1/4$-inch diagonal
     rounds

$1/4$ cup light olive oil

$1/2$ teaspoon salt

$1/2$ teaspoon freshly ground pepper

     Cherry Tomato Salsa
     (recipe follows)

Using a pastry brush, lightly coat all
the vegetables with olive oil and season
with salt and pepper.

Preheat a grill pan over medium heat
until very hot. Add all the vegetables and
cook for about 4 minutes. Brush with
a little more olive oil, turn, and cook for
4 minutes more. Transfer to warm plates
and serve with Cherry Tomato Salsa.

Cherry Tomato Salsa

1 cup red cherry tomatoes, halved

1 cup yellow cherry tomatoes, halved

2 tablespoons finely diced red onion

1 tablespoon minced jalapeño chile

2 tablespoons fresh lime juice

$1/4$ cup coarsely chopped fresh cilantro

1 tablespoon chili powder

$1/4$ teaspoon salt

$1/4$ teaspoon freshly ground pepper

In a medium glass or nonreactive metal bowl, combine the tomatoes, onion, chile, lime juice, cilantro, chili powder, salt, and pepper. Let sit, loosely covered, for at least 1 hour. (The salsa can also be made up to four hours ahead, covered tightly, and refrigerated. Bring to room temperature before use.)

I first tasted small, sweet cipolline onions fresh from a garden in Verona in Northern Italy. They are just larger than pearl onions but smaller than yellow onions, and are now available at most gourmet food markets. They also make remarkable creamed onions.

Summer Vegetables with
Cherry Tomato Salsa

THIS SANDWICH IS A PERFECT EXAMPLE OF THE MAGIC THE
GRILL PAN WORKS ON VEGETABLES. TRY IT AS AN OPEN-
FACE SANDWICH OR EVEN AN ANTIPASTO. THIS IS DEFINITELY
ONE OF MY PERSONAL FAVORITES.

Mediterranean Vegetable Sandwich

SERVES 2 AS AN APPETIZER OR A LIGHT MEAL

1 medium red bell pepper,
cored, seeded, and cut into
$1/2$-inch strips

1 medium eggplant, peeled and
cut into $1/2$-inch-thick slices

1 medium zucchini, cut into
$1/8$-inch-thick slices

1 medium portobello mushroom,
gills and stem removed and
sliced into $1/4$-inch-thick strips

$1/4$ cup light olive oil

2 sandwich-sized slices focaccia,
halved lengthwise

1 cup sliced or shredded
mozzarella cheese

8 large fresh basil leaves

With a pastry brush, lightly coat the
vegetables with the olive oil.

Preheat a grill pan over medium heat
until very hot. Transfer all the vegetables
to the pan and grill about 3 minutes
on each side, or until softened. Transfer
to a cutting board or plate. Place the focaccia slices in the grill pan cut side down
and toast for 2 to 3 minutes, or until
slightly charred. Divide the mozzarella on
2 slices of focaccia. Divide and stack
equal amounts of the eggplant, zucchini,
mushroom, and bell pepper on the 2
slices, top with equal portions of the basil,
and then cover with the remaining two
slices of focaccia. Serve immediately.

The portobello mushroom is
a large brown mushroom with an
open cap. It is essential that
the stems and gills be removed.
Sadly, I have never met a chef
(or even a home cook) who
removes the gills from these
mushrooms. It is a mostly forgot-
ten practice that is dying with
an older generation of Italian
chefs. Although the mushroom
tastes good either way, once
you try it without the gills you
will understand what a difference
this makes.

Surprisingly, my favorite tool
when removing the gills from the
mushrooms is a melon baller.
Although you may use a spoon,
a melon baller has sharp edges
and will gently scrape away
the gills, leaving the delicate
white flesh. At this point all it will
need is a brush of light olive
oil and a little salt and pepper.

WHEN SERVED OVER BASMATI RICE, THESE KABOBS MAKE
A COMPLETE MEAL FOR THE VEGETARIAN AT YOUR TABLE. TO
PLEASE THE MEAT EATERS, MAKE THIS RECIPE ALONG
WITH ANOTHER KABOB RECIPE SUCH AS THE GARLIC CHICKEN
KABOBS ON ROSEMARY SKEWERS (PAGE 97) OR THE BEEF
KABOBS WITH ASIAN MARINADE (PAGE 83).

Vegetable Kabobs with Lemon-Herb Basting Sauce

SERVES 2 (3 KABOBS EACH) AS A MAIN COURSE

BASTING SAUCE

$1/_4$ cup light olive oil

6 large cloves Roasted Garlic
(recipe follows)

4 teaspoons minced fresh thyme or
2 teaspoons dried thyme, crumbled

$1/_2$ cup fresh lemon juice

———

6 wooden skewers, soaked
in water for 15 minutes

1 large zucchini,
cut into 2-inch cubes

2 large crookneck squash,
cut into 2-inch cubes

12 cherry tomatoes

12 button mushrooms, brushed off

12 pearl onions, peeled

2 Anaheim chiles,
seeded and cut into 2-inch pieces

To make the basting sauce:

In a small glass or nonreactive metal bowl,
combine the oil, garlic, thyme, and
lemon juice. Whisk together until smooth.

Skewer the vegetables, alternating to
create an attractive arrangement.

Preheat a grill pan over medium heat until
very hot. Using a pastry brush, lightly
coat the kabobs with the basting sauce.
Add to the pan and cook for 3 minutes,
basting frequently. Turn and cook for
3 minutes more. Serve immediately.

RAW GARLIC IS COMMONLY USED IN MAKING SALAD DRESSINGS. HOWEVER, I PERSONALLY SELDOM USE RAW GARLIC BECAUSE OF ITS BITTER TASTE AND PUNGENT ODOR. ROASTED GARLIC IS A STAPLE IN MY KITCHEN BECAUSE IT AFFORDS THE SWEETER TASTE OF GARLIC AND DOES NOT LEAVE A FOUL TASTE IN YOUR MOUTH. THE GARLIC CLOVES BECOME SO SOFT WHEN ROASTED THAT THEY CAN ACTUALLY BE SPREAD ON CRACKERS OR BREAD.

Roasted Garlic

garlic cloves, peeled

olive oil

Fill an oven-safe dish halfway with peeled garlic cloves, and cover completely with olive oil. Bake at 350°F for 20 minutes. Remove from the oven and let the mixture cool, uncovered, until room temperature. Store in a glass mason jar or similar airtight container in the pantry for up to one month.

YOUR CLOCK IS THE MOST ESSENTIAL INGREDIENT FOR
THE SUCCESS OF THIS TREAT: GRILL THE BREAD FOR 3 MINUTES
EXACTLY OR IT WILL GET TOO CRUNCHY.

Bruschetta

SERVES 2 AS AN APPETIZER

5 large, ripe plum tomatoes

$1/3$ cup finely chopped red onion

$1/4$ cup finely chopped cilantro

2 teaspoons fresh lime juice

3 cloves Roasted Garlic (page 29)

$1/4$ teaspoon salt

$1/4$ teaspoon freshly ground pepper

6 $1/4$-inch-thick slices of crusty baguette

2 tablespoons light olive oil

Halve the tomatoes lengthwise and remove the seeds. Cut the flesh into $1/4$-inch dice and place in a medium glass or nonreactive metal bowl. Add the onion, cilantro, lime juice, garlic, salt, and pepper, and stir together gently. Let sit, loosely covered, at room temperature for 1 hour. (The tomato mixture can be made and kept in the refrigerator for up to 4 hours. Bring to room temperature before using.)

Preheat a grill pan over medium heat until very hot. Brush the bread slices with olive oil on one side and place them in the grill pan oiled side down. Cook for 3 minutes, then transfer to plates, grilled side up. Using a slotted spoon, top the bread slices with the tomato mixture.

There is no better way to prepare eggplant than in the grill pan. I use Western eggplant in this recipe. It is available at most supermarkets, has a deep purple skin, and is egg shaped. Other varieties can be used, including Japanese, white, and baby eggplant. Crumbling dried herbs between your fingertips releases the fragrant oils and improves the flavor of the herbs dramatically.

Eggplant Parmesan

SERVES 2 AS A SIDE DISH OR 4 AS AN APPETIZER

1 medium eggplant, about
1 $^1\!/_2$ pounds, top trimmed

1 teaspoon salt

1 teaspoon dried oregano,
crumbled

1 teaspoon dried basil, crumbled

$^1\!/_4$ teaspoon freshly ground pepper

$^1\!/_2$ cup light olive oil

$^1\!/_2$ cup fresh or prepared
tomato sauce

1 cup shredded mozzarella cheese

$^1\!/_4$ cup grated Parmesan cheese

Cut the eggplant into $^1\!/_4$-inch-thick slices. Arrange the slices in a single layer on paper towels. Sprinkle the eggplant with half of the salt and let stand for 1 hour. In a small bowl, combine the dried herbs, pepper, and remaining salt.

Preheat a grill pan over medium heat until very hot. Pat the eggplant dry with paper towels and transfer to a cutting board. Brush one side of the eggplant with olive oil and season with half of the herb mixture. Transfer to the hot grill pan seasoned side down. Brush the other side with olive oil and season with the remaining herb mixture. Cook for 5 minutes and turn. Spoon about 1 teaspoon of the tomato sauce onto each slice of eggplant and top with the cheeses. Cook for an additional 2 minutes, or until the cheese has almost melted. Serve immediately.

THE ONLY MEMBER OF THE ONION FAMILY I ENJOY AS
MUCH AS SHALLOTS IS THE VIDALIA ONION. SHALLOTS ARE A
STAPLE IN MY KITCHEN, AND I USE THEM AS I DO VIDALIA
ONIONS, TO SWEETEN EVERYTHING FROM SAUCES TO SALADS TO
SALSAS. THIS IS AN IDEAL SIDE DISH FOR LAMB CHOPS
WITH LEMON AND ROSEMARY (PAGE 66).

Glazed Shallots

SERVES 2 AS A SIDE DISH

10 shallots, peeled and halved
   lengthwise

2 tablespoons light olive oil

$1/4$ teaspoon salt

$1/4$ teaspoon freshly ground pepper

Preheat a grill pan over medium heat until very hot. Using a pastry brush, lightly coat the cut sides of the shallots with olive oil and season with salt and pepper. Cook, cut side down, for 4 minutes. Brush the top side with olive oil and season with salt and pepper. Turn the shallots and cook for 2 minutes more, or until they are golden and tender.

THE WILD BOAR BACON IN THIS RECIPE COMES FROM HOUSE OF SMOKE (SEE MAIL-ORDER SOURCES, PAGE 103), THE FINEST PURVEYOR OF WILD GAME MEATS I HAVE EVER FOUND. THE BACON IS VERY MEATY AND WHEN COOKED IT RESEMBLES SLICED HAM. THIS VERY UNUSUAL INGREDIENT GIVES A CLASSIC DISH SOME CONTEMPORARY FLAIR. YOU MAY SUBSTITUTE A GOOD-QUALITY APPLEWOOD-SMOKED PORK BACON FOR THE WILD BOAR BACON.

New Potatoes with Hickory-Smoked Wild Boar Bacon

SERVES 2 AS A SIDE DISH

1 pound golf ball–sized
new potatoes

1/4 pound hickory-smoked wild boar
bacon slab or applewood-smoked
pork bacon, sliced into thin strips

Blanch potatoes in salted boiling water for 10 minutes, or until tender but not falling apart or mushy. Cut in half.

Preheat a grill pan over medium heat until very hot. Add potatoes and bacon to the grill pan. Cook about 10 minutes, turning frequently. Serve immediately.

THESE ARE A SUMMER FAVORITE AND A COMPLEMENT TO
ANY MEAL. TRY THIS RECIPE WITH LINDSEY'S LONDON BROIL
(PAGE 69) OR ANY ASIAN-STYLE MAIN COURSE. BE SURE
NOT TO OVERCOOK THE PEA PODS. THEY SHOULD BE GRILLED
JUST UNTIL THEY SURRENDER THEIR SWEET NATURAL
SUGAR WHILE REMAINING CRUNCHY.

Sugar Snap Peas with Garlic

SERVES 2 AS A SIDE DISH

$1/2$ pound sugar snap peas,
   strings removed and ends trimmed

2 cloves garlic, crushed

1 tablespoon light olive oil

Preheat a grill pan over medium heat until very hot. In a small bowl, toss the snap peas, garlic, and oil together. Add to the pan and cook, turning frequently, for about 4 minutes, or until just tender. Discard the garlic and serve immediately.

SEAFOOD

Just the number of cooking options for seafood can be intimidating. Should you broil, poach, bake, fry, or sauté? With a grill pan you can sear ahi tuna, get a perfect crust on a salmon steak, and even serve up a succulent lobster tail. Go ahead . . . enjoy the fruits of the sea with confidence!

WHILE ON FISHING TRIPS OFF THE COAST OF CABO SAN LUCAS, I AM USUALLY ABLE TO SECURE MY SHARE OF TUNA. THIS FAST FISH TRAVELS ONE OF THE MOST SCENIC ROUTES IN THE WORLD, FROM THE SEA OF CORTEZ, LOOPING AROUND THE TIP OF BAJA AND UP THE COAST TO THE PACIFIC NORTHWEST, AND THEN BACK AGAIN. AFTER A HOT DAY IN THE SUN FIGHTING FOR DINNER, ONLY SUSHI AND THIS SALAD CAN SATISFY MY SEAFOOD CRAVINGS.

Deep Sea Lightning Salad

SERVES 2 AS A MAIN COURSE

4 golf ball–sized new potatoes

2 6-ounce tuna steaks, brought to room temperature before cooking

5 teaspoons light olive oil

$^1/_4$ teaspoon salt

$^1/_4$ teaspoon freshly ground pepper

2 cups mesclun or mixed baby lettuce leaves

$^1/_4$ cup Basil Vinaigrette (recipe follows)

1 Haas avocado, peeled and thinly sliced

1 medium tomato, cored and cut into quarters

1 tablespoon Niçoise olives

1 tablespoon capers, drained

1 2-ounce can anchovy fillets

Blanch potatoes in salted boiling water for 10 minutes, or until tender but not falling apart or mushy. Cut in half.

Preheat a grill pan over medium heat until very hot. Brush each tuna steak with 2 teaspoons of the oil and season both sides to taste with salt and pepper. Grill to desired doneness (2 minutes for rare, 3 $^1/_2$ minutes for medium, and 5 minutes for well done, turning once). Remove fish and set aside, loosely covered.

Brush the potatoes with remaining 1 teaspoon of oil. Grill for about 2 minutes, turning with tongs to char lightly but evenly.

In a glass or nonreactive metal bowl, toss the greens with about half the vinaigrette. Add the avocado, tomato, olives, and potatoes and toss together gently.

For each serving, place 1 tuna steak on a large plate and drizzle with a little vinaigrette. Surround the tuna with the salad, dividing all the ingredients evenly. Scatter the capers over each salad and drape the anchovies over the top.

Basil Vinaigrette

MAKES ABOUT 1 CUP

2 cups loosely packed basil leaves

2 teaspoons red wine vinegar

1 tablespoon fresh lime juice

1 tablespoon chopped red onion

$^1/_2$ teaspoon salt

$^1/_4$ teaspoon freshly ground pepper

$^1/_2$ cup light olive oil

In a food processor or blender, combine basil, vinegar, lime juice, onion, salt, and pepper, and purée. With the motor running, slowly add the oil until emulsified, scraping down the sides as necessary. Transfer to a squeeze bottle. (The vinaigrette may be made up to a day ahead and refrigerated. Bring to room temperature before serving.)

Deep Sea Lightning Salad

THIS CURRY CAN BE USED ON ANY WHITE FISH, SHRIMP,
OR CHICKEN. I RECOMMEND WASHING THE FOOD PROCESSOR
OR BLENDER IMMEDIATELY AFTER MIXING THE CURRY
TO AVOID SEASONING THE BOWL. ALSO, USE RUBBER GLOVES
OR TONGS WHEN HANDLING THE SHRIMP SO THAT THE
TURMERIC DOES NOT STAIN YOUR HANDS.

Crispy Halibut
with Green Curry Prawns

SERVES 4 AS A MAIN COURSE

1 bunch (about 2 cups) roughly
  chopped cilantro, a few whole
  leaves reserved for garnish

3 cloves garlic, peeled

1–2 small dried red chiles,
  or to taste, stemmed and seeded

1 teaspoon ground turmeric

1 teaspoon curry powder

1 tablespoon sugar

1/4 teaspoon salt

3 tablespoons fish sauce or nam pla
  (see note opposite page)

3 tablespoons coconut cream
  (see note opposite page)

8 large prawns,
  shelled and deveined

4 6-ounce halibut steaks
  (about 3/4 inch thick)

Salt and freshly ground pepper

1 lime, quartered

In a food processor or blender, combine
the cilantro, garlic, chiles, spices, sugar,
and salt and process to a coarse paste. Add
the fish sauce and coconut cream and
pulse again until very smooth.

Reserve 1/4 cup of the curry mixture for
garnish and transfer the remaining
curry mixture to a glass or nonreactive
metal bowl. Add the prawns and turn to
coat them evenly. Cover and let the
prawns marinate at room temperature for
1 hour, turning occasionally.

Season the halibut to taste with salt and
pepper.

Preheat a grill pan over medium heat
until very hot. Add the fish and grill until
just starting to become opaque in the
center, about 3 minutes. Turn the fish
and, using a slotted spoon to remove them
from the curry mixture, add the prawns
to the pan. Grill the prawns for about
1 1/2 minutes on each side, by which time
the halibut will be done.

Transfer the fish to warm plates and top
with the prawns. For the final touch,
garnish with the reserved cilantro leaves,
lime wedges, and a drizzle of the remaining curry mixture.

Nam pla is a salty, fermented
fish sauce and is available
in bottles at most gourmet food
stores and Asian markets.
Coconut cream is unlike coconut
milk; it can be found in the liquor
section of most supermarkets.
Coconut cream is the main
ingredient used to make piña
coladas. My favorite brand
is Pepe Lopez.

THIS FISH BRINGS BACK SO MANY UNDERWATER MEMORIES! WHILE WORKING AS A PRIVATE CHEF ON A YACHT, WE WOULD GO TO A REMOTE ISLAND IN THE CARIBBEAN SEA, WHERE I WOULD SKIN DIVE FOR GROUPER ALL DAY, SPEARING TWO OR THREE FISH AT A TIME. WHEN THE SUN STARTED TO FADE, THE GROUPER WOULD START TO COOK. THIS FISH TASTES LIKE DELICATE LOBSTER MEAT AND CAN BE ACCOMPANIED BY ALMOST ANY SAUCE. GROUPER IS TRULY THE CHICKEN OF THE SEA IN THE CARIBBEAN.

Avis Island Grouper

SERVES 2 AS A MAIN COURSE

2 skinless, boneless grouper fillets
(about 6 ounces each) or other
lean, firm white fish fillets

1 tablespoon superfine flour
(such as Wondra)

$1/4$ teaspoon salt

$1/4$ teaspoon freshly ground pepper

2 slices smoked bacon

Preheat a grill pan over medium heat until very hot. Lightly dust both sides of the grouper with the flour and season with salt and pepper. Add the bacon to the pan and cook until the fat starts to turn transparent. Remove the bacon from the pan and discard. Add the grouper and cook for about 7 minutes, or until golden. Turn and cook for 4 minutes more. Transfer to warm plates and serve immediately.

My friend Louie, a magnificent Pacific Rim chef, inspired this very decadent dish. We were doing a live cooking show together, and when he poured balsamic vinegar over strawberries the audience cringed. Their attitude changed when they tasted it. The sweetness of the season's best strawberries combined with the fine aged Orange-Rosemary Balsamic Vinegar from Bittersweet Herb Farm (see mail-order sources, page 103) produces an unbeatable flavor. The key is to allow the strawberries to marinate for only 15 minutes.

Salmon with Balsamic Strawberries

SERVES 2 AS A MAIN COURSE

1 cup strawberries, wiped clean, hulled, and halved lengthwise

1 cup Orange-Rosemary Balsamic Vinegar or any good-quality balsamic vinegar

2 6-ounce salmon steaks (about $1/2$ inch thick)

$1/4$ teaspoon salt

$1/4$ teaspoon freshly ground pepper

In a small glass or nonreactive metal bowl, combine the strawberries and balsamic vinegar. Let stand for 15 minutes.

Preheat a grill pan over medium heat until very hot. Season both sides of the salmon with salt and pepper. Add to the pan and cook for 4 minutes on one side. Turn and cook for 4 minutes more. Transfer the salmon to warm plates. Using a slotted spoon, remove the strawberries from the vinegar and spoon over the salmon. Discard the remaining vinegar. Serve immediately.

EVERY YEAR BEGINNING IN MAY, I START LOOKING FOR SOFT-SHELL CRAB IN THE GOURMET MARKETS. ALTHOUGH THIS TYPE OF CRAB IS COMMONLY FOUND DEEP-FRIED IN JAPANESE RESTAURANTS, THE GRILL-PAN METHOD BETTER ENABLES YOU TO TASTE THE SWEETNESS OF THIS DELICATE MEAT.

Soft-Shell Crab on Arugula with Sun-Dried Tomatoes

SERVES 2 AS A MAIN COURSE

4 medium soft-shell crabs, cleaned

Milk, for soaking

$1/4$ cup light olive oil

$1/4$ teaspoon salt

$1/4$ teaspoon freshly ground pepper

4 cups arugula, tough stems removed, washed and dried

$1/2$ cup oil-packed sun-dried tomatoes, drained and coarsely chopped

Lemon Beurre Blanc (recipe follows)

Soak the crabs in milk for one hour, then gently rinse them under cold running water and pat dry with a paper towel. Lightly brush the shells of the crabs with olive oil and season them with salt and pepper.

Preheat a grill pan over medium heat until very hot. Add the crabs shell side down and grill for 4 minutes. Brush the underside of the crabs with olive oil, season with salt and pepper, and turn them over. Grill them for 4 minutes more.

In a medium glass or nonreactive metal bowl, toss the arugula with the sun-dried tomatoes. The oil remaining on the tomatoes will lightly coat the arugula. Move the soft-shell crabs to the edge of the pan, turn off the heat, and add the arugula mixture to the pan. Toss gently and place equal amounts of the arugula mixture in the center of two warm dinner plates. Top each with two of the crabs and drizzle with Lemon Beurre Blanc.

Lemon Beurre Blanc

1 1/2 tablespoons finely chopped shallots

2 tablespoons white wine vinegar

1 1/2 tablespoons dry vermouth

2 tablespoons fresh lemon juice

1/2 cup heavy whipping cream

1 cup unsalted butter, cut into small pieces, at room temperature

1/2 teaspoon salt

1/4 teaspoon ground white pepper

In a small saucepan, combine the shallots, vinegar, vermouth, and lemon juice. Bring to a simmer over medium-high heat and cook until the liquid is almost gone, 3 to 4 minutes. Reduce the heat to medium, stir in the cream, and cook until the mixture thickens, about 2 minutes. Remove the pan from the heat and set it aside until you are ready to serve. Just before serving, place the saucepan over low heat and stir until heated through. Add the butter, salt, and pepper. Whisk constantly until the butter has melted and emulsified into the sauce. Serve immediately.

47

Soft-Shell Crab on Arugula
with Sun-Dried Tomatoes

THIS MAKES A HEALTHY AND COLORFUL MEAL WHEN
ACCOMPANIED BY RICE, OR YOU CAN PLACE THE FISH ON
A BED OF GREENS AND USE THE SALSA AS A DRESSING
FOR AN APPEALING AND ATTRACTIVE MAIN-COURSE SALAD.

Swordfish with Avocado Salsa

SERVES 2 AS A MAIN COURSE

Avocado Salsa

- 1 Haas avocado, peeled and coarsely chopped
- 1 medium tomato, coarsely chopped
- 1 tablespoon finely diced red onion
- 2 teaspoons finely diced jalapeño chile
- 2 tablespoons fresh lime juice
- $1/4$ cup coarsely chopped cilantro
- $1/4$ teaspoon salt
- $1/4$ teaspoon freshly ground pepper

- 2 6-ounce swordfish steaks, brought to room temperature before cooking
- 2 teaspoons light olive oil

  Salt and freshly ground pepper

To make the salsa:

Combine the avocado, tomato, onion, jalapeño, lime juice, and cilantro in a glass or nonreactive metal bowl. Toss together gently. Add the salt and pepper, cover, and refrigerate for up to 2 hours. Bring to room temperature before serving.

Preheat a grill pan over medium heat until very hot. Brush the steaks with olive oil and season to taste with salt and pepper. Grill for 4 to 6 minutes on each side, or until golden. Transfer to warm plates and top with salsa. Serve immediately.

SEA BASS IS A RELATIVELY OILY FISH. AS YOU GRILL IT THE
NATURAL JUICES WILL MOISTEN THE OUTSIDE AND, AS
THE FISH HEATS UP, THE OUTSIDE WILL BECOME GOLDEN BROWN
AND CRUNCHY. I USE KEY LIMES IN THIS RECIPE, BUT THE
MORE WIDELY AVAILABLE PERSIAN LIMES CAN BE USED INSTEAD.

Key Lime Sea Bass with Toasted Leeks

SERVES 2 AS A MAIN COURSE

2 6-ounce sea bass fillets

$^1/_4$ teaspoon salt

$^1/_4$ teaspoon freshly ground pepper

2 tablespoons grated lime zest

$^1/_4$ cup fresh Key lime juice

2 teaspoons finely grated
   fresh ginger

1 tablespoon honey

2 medium leeks, white and light
   green parts only, thinly sliced

1 tablespoon light olive oil

Season the sea bass with salt and pepper and set aside. In a small glass or non-reactive metal bowl, combine the lime zest, lime juice, ginger, and honey. Stir together to make a paste. Rub the paste on the sea bass and let it sit, loosely covered, for 30 minutes.

In a colander, rinse leeks well, separating them into individual rings. Dry the leeks thoroughly and toss them with the olive oil.

Preheat a grill pan over medium heat until very hot. Add the sea bass and the leeks at the same time, on opposite sides of the pan. Using tongs, toss the leeks frequently. Cook the sea bass until nicely browned, about 4 minutes. Turn and cook for 4 minutes more. Transfer the fish to two warm plates and top with the leeks. Serve immediately.

SLOWLY CARAMELIZED BY THE HEAT OF THE GRILL PAN,
THIS GINGER-SPIKED MIXTURE OF HONEY, ORANGE JUICE, LEMON
JUICE, AND SOY SAUCE FORMS A LIP-SMACKING GLAZE ON
THE SALMON STEAKS. IF YOU CANNOT FIND HARICOTS VERTS,
YOU CAN USE BLANCHED GREEN BEANS.

Orange-Soy Glazed Salmon with Haricots Verts and Red Onion

SERVES 2 AS A MAIN COURSE

$1/2$ cup orange juice

$1/4$ cup honey

$1/4$ cup soy sauce

2 tablespoons fresh lemon juice

$1/2$ teaspoon ground ginger

2 6-ounce salmon steaks,
$1/2$ inch thick

$1/4$ pound haricots verts or thin
green beans, washed and trimmed

1 small red onion, thinly sliced

2 teaspoons light olive oil

In a baking dish, combine the orange juice, honey, soy sauce, lemon juice, and ginger. Add the salmon steaks and turn to coat evenly with the glaze. Let stand, covered, at room temperature for 1 hour.

Gently toss haricots verts and red onion with the olive oil.

Preheat a grill pan over medium heat until very hot. Place the salmon steaks on one side of the grill pan and put the haricots verts and red onion on the other side. Using tongs, toss the beans and onion frequently for 4 minutes. Remove the vegetables and transfer to warm plates. Turn the salmon and grill for 4 minutes more. Transfer the salmon to the warm plates and serve.

I HAVE OFTEN THOUGHT THAT I COULD LIVE ON THIS DISH
AS MY SOLE SOURCE OF PROTEIN. IF YOU ARE A FAN OF SUSHI,
I ENCOURAGE YOU TO ENJOY THIS DISH RARE.

Seared Ahi Tuna with Wasabi Sauce

SERVES 2 AS A MAIN COURSE

1 teaspoon wasabi paste

$1/4$ teaspoon grated fresh ginger

$1/4$ cup low-sodium soy sauce

2 6-ounce, sushi-grade ahi tuna
steaks, brought to room
temperature before cooking

2 tablespoons light olive oil

Salt and freshly ground pepper

Zest of one lemon,
removed with a zester

To make the sauce, in a small glass or nonreactive metal bowl whisk together the wasabi, ginger, and soy sauce until well blended. Let stand at room temperature.

Preheat a grill pan over medium heat until very hot. Rub the steaks with the olive oil and season to taste with salt and pepper. Grill each side for 2 minutes, then hold with tongs to grill the edges for 1 minute on each side (for rare). Transfer the tuna to a cutting board and slice into $1/4$-inch crosswise strips. Transfer the strips to two plates and drizzle the wasabi sauce over the top. Garnish with lemon zest.

THIS DISH IS EXCITING AS AN APPETIZER OR AS A MAIN DISH
OVER PASTA. I RECOMMEND SERVING IT WITH CRUSTY
BREAD TO SOAK UP THE JUICE. TAKE A LITTLE EXTRA TIME AND
CLEAN THE MUSSELS VERY WELL, MAKING SURE TO REMOVE
THE "BEARDS" OR HAIR ATTACHED AT ONE END.

Garlic Grilled Mussels

SERVES 2 AS A MAIN COURSE OR 4 AS AN APPETIZER

1 pound black mussels (about 3 dozen), scrubbed and debearded

3 cloves garlic, crushed

1/2 cup finely chopped red onion

1/2 cup dry white wine

1 teaspoon arrowroot

1/3 cup fresh lemon juice

1/2 tablespoon unsalted butter, cut in half

1/4 cup finely chopped parsley

Soak the mussels in a bowl of cold water or in a sink for 30 minutes. Any sand will come out and sink to the bottom of the bowl.

Preheat a grill pan over medium heat until very hot. Add the garlic, onion, and wine. Simmer for 5 minutes. Add the mussels and simmer for an additional 5 minutes. All mussels should be open by that time. Any mussels that have not opened after 8 minutes should be discarded. With a slotted spoon, remove the mussels from the pan and place on a platter. Cover with foil and set aside.

Whisk the arrowroot into the lemon juice and add to the grill pan. Add the butter and jiggle the pan to melt the butter and incorporate it into the sauce. Pour the sauce over the mussels and sprinkle the parsley over the top. Serve immediately.

THIS DISH IS A DELICIOUS EXAMPLE OF THE VERSATILITY
A GRILL PAN OFFERS YOU. IT WILL ENCOURAGE YOU TO TRY
OTHER FISH FILLETS THAT MIGHT TYPICALLY FALL APART
ON A TRADITIONAL GRILL.

Red Snapper with Spicy Aïoli

SERVES 2 AS A MAIN COURSE

SPICY AÏOLI

1 cup prepared mayonnaise

1 clove Roasted Garlic
(see page 29)

1 tablespoon canned diced
green chiles

2 tablespoons fresh lime juice

1/4 teaspoon salt

1/2 teaspoon freshly ground pepper

1 tablespoon finely chopped
green onions (white part only)

———

2 6-ounce red snapper fillets

1 tablespoon light olive oil

1/4 teaspoon salt

1/4 teaspoon freshly ground pepper

To make the aïoli:

In a food processor or blender, combine the mayonnaise, roasted garlic, green chiles, lime juice, salt, and pepper. Purée until smooth. (The aïoli may be prepared up to 1 day ahead and stored in an airtight container in the refrigerator. Bring to room temperature before use.)

Preheat a grill pan over medium heat until very hot. Lightly brush the red snapper fillets with olive oil and season both sides with salt and pepper. Place in the grill pan and cook for 3 minutes. Turn and cook for 3 minutes more. Transfer to warm plates and top with spicy aïoli and green onions.

PRESENTED ON A BED OF GREENS, THIS FIRM, LEAN FISH
DRESSED WITH A REFRESHING, FRUITY VINAIGRETTE
MAKES AN IMPRESSIVE MAIN-COURSE SALAD. OR PAIR IT WITH
RICE AND VEGETABLES FOR A SPECIAL DINNER FOR TWO.

Mahimahi with Citrus-Raspberry Vinaigrette

SERVES 2 AS A MAIN COURSE

CITRUS-RASPBERRY VINAIGRETTE

1 tablespoon fresh orange juice

1 tablespoon fresh lemon juice

1 tablespoon fresh lime juice

1 tablespoon raspberry vinegar

$1/4$ cup light olive oil

1 tablespoon minced red onion

1 tablespoon minced red bell pepper

$1/4$ teaspoon salt

$1/4$ teaspoon freshly ground pepper

———

2 6-ounce mahimahi fillets

Salt and freshly ground pepper

To make the vinaigrette:

In a food processor or blender, combine the orange juice, lemon juice, lime juice, and vinegar. With the motor running, slowly add the olive oil and continue processing until emulsified. Transfer the mixture to a small glass or nonreactive metal bowl and stir in the red onion, bell pepper, salt, and pepper to taste. This vinaigrette may be prepared 1 day in advance and refrigerated in an airtight container.

Season both sides of the mahimahi with salt and pepper.

Preheat a grill pan over medium heat until very hot. Place the fillets in the grill pan and cook for 4 minutes on each side, or until golden brown. Transfer the fillets to two warm dinner plates and drizzle with Citrus-Raspberry Vinaigrette.

———

WHILE I WAS A CHEF IN THE CARIBBEAN, SLIPPER LOBSTER WAS A STAPLE IN MY KITCHEN. I HUNTED ALMOST EVERY DAY, AND WHEN I COULD NOT SPEAR A DELICIOUS GROUPER I WOULD BE FORCED TO SERVE LOBSTER. ALTHOUGH THIS DOESN'T SOUND LIKE A TRAGEDY, SLIPPER LOBSTER IS NOT AS SWEET AS MAINE LOBSTER AND DEMANDS CREATIVE COOKING TECHNIQUES. THE FIRST TIME THAT I MADE THIS DISH IN A GRILL PAN THE MEAT WAS SO MOIST AND SWEET I KNEW I WOULD NEVER MAKE LOBSTER ANY OTHER WAY.

Lobster Tails with Roasted Garlic

SERVES 2 AS A MAIN COURSE

2 lobster tails,
   about $^1/_2$ pound each

5 cloves Roasted Garlic (page 29)

$^1/_4$ cup light olive oil

$^1/_4$ teaspoon salt

$^1/_4$ teaspoon freshly ground pepper

Split the lobster tails down the middle lengthwise. Combine the garlic and olive oil in a small food processor or blender, and purée until smooth. Using a pastry brush, coat the cut sides of the lobster tails with the garlic mixture. Season with salt and pepper.

Preheat a grill pan over medium heat until very hot. Place the lobster tails in the grill pan cut side down and cook for 6 minutes. Turn the lobster and cook shell side down for 2 minutes. Lightly brush the cut side with more of the garlic mixture and season again with salt and pepper. Turn and cook with the cut side down for 2 minutes more. Transfer the lobster to warm plates and serve.

THIS IS ONE OF MY FAVORITE PARTY SNACKS. THE SPICES FROM
THE LITTLE CAJUN ANDOUILLETTE SAUSAGES SEASON THE
SHRIMP AS THEY COOK TOGETHER ON THE SKEWERS. IN FACT,
THERE IS NO NEED FOR ADDITIONAL OILS OR SEASONINGS.
THE SKEWERS CAN BE ASSEMBLED IN THE MORNING AND GRILLED
THAT NIGHT, MAKING THIS DISH EXTREMELY EASY.

Cajun Shrimp and Andouillette Sausage Skewers

SERVES 2 AS AN APPETIZER

4 wooden or metal skewers

10 large shrimp, peeled and deveined

12 andouillette sausages (see note)
   or any small, flavorful sausage

If you are using wooden skewers, soak them in water for 15 minutes before using.

Thread the meat onto the skewers, alternating the shrimp and sausage.

Preheat a grill pan over medium heat until very hot. Place the skewers in the pan and cook for 5 minutes. Turn and cook for 5 minutes more. Transfer to warm plates. Serve immediately.

Andouillette sausage is a French-style tripe sausage, and is available at most gourmet butcher shops.

MEATS

Growing up in Kentucky, beef, pork, and game were a significant part of our diet. As a young girl and an anxious cook, making roasts, pork tenderloin, and stew was as common as the mashed potatoes we served with them. It became apparent at a young age that the task of barbecuing steaks, ribs, and chops was reserved for the male gender. Even when I tried it, the heat and smoke from the open fire discouraged me. It seemed as though the consensus became the law; there was not one woman who was highly regarded for her grilling expertise. However, the grill pan makes open-fire cooking seem archaic, and by softening the flame, turns the act of cooking meat into a more delicate adventure—an experience perhaps everyone now can enjoy.

I WAS AT A BARBECUE WITH A GROUP OF FRIENDS IN NORTHERN ITALY ONE FINE EVENING. THEY WERE GRILLING LAMB CHOPS RUBBED WITH LEMON AND ROSEMARY. THE LAMB CHOPS WERE SO GUTSY AND BOLD THAT I WAS INSPIRED TO TRY THEM ON MY OWN. TO MY DELIGHT, THEY WERE EVEN BETTER COOKED IN A GRILL PAN. MAKE SURE YOU HAVE GOOD VENTILATION WHEN YOU MAKE THIS DISH—NO MATTER HOW YOU COOK IT, LAMB HAS A VERY STRONG SMELL.

Lamb Chops with Lemon and Rosemary

SERVES 2 AS A MAIN COURSE

6 loin lamb chops (1 $1/2$ inches thick), rinsed and patted dry

$1/4$ cup fresh lemon juice

$1/4$ cup fresh rosemary sprigs

$1/4$ teaspoon salt

$1/4$ teaspoon freshly ground pepper

Preheat a grill pan over medium heat until very hot. Using a pastry brush, lightly coat both sides of the chops with lemon juice and season with half of the rosemary, salt, and pepper. Add to the pan and grill for 4 minutes. Brush with lemon juice and season with the remaining rosemary, salt, and pepper. Turn and grill for 4 minutes more (for rare), or to your liking. Transfer the chops to a warm platter and let stand, loosely covered, for 3 minutes before serving.

IN [?]PES IN THIS BOOK I GAVE GRILL [?]AL OF MY FRIENDS AND [?]GING THEM TO TRY MY RECIPES AS [?]N. MY PERSONAL ASSISTANT, [?] THIS RECIPE, APOLOGIZING FOR ITS SIMPLICITY BUT RAVING ABOUT THE FLAVOR. I TRIED IT AND CONCLUDED THAT SOMETIMES THE SIMPLICITY OF A RECIPE IS WHAT MAKES IT WORTHWHILE. TRY THIS RECIPE WITH SUGAR SNAP PEAS WITH GARLIC (PAGE 35).

Lindsey's London Broil

SERVES 2 AS A MAIN COURSE

$1/2$ cup light olive oil

$1/4$ cup low-sodium soy sauce

$1/4$ cup red wine vinegar

2 tablespoons crushed garlic

1 London broil or flank steak
(8 to 12 ounces)

To make the marinade, stir together the olive oil, soy sauce, vinegar, and garlic in a shallow baking dish. Place the meat in the dish and turn to coat both sides. Refrigerate, tightly covered, for at least 6 hours or overnight, turning at least once. Remove the meat from the refrigerator and allow it to come to room temperature for about 45 minutes.

Preheat a grill pan over medium heat until very hot. Drain the marinade from the baking dish and transfer the meat to the grill pan. Cook for 4 minutes, then turn and cook 4 minutes more for medium rare, 6 minutes for medium. Transfer the meat to a cutting board and cover loosely with foil. Let rest for about 4 minutes. Thinly slice the meat across the grain. Serve immediately.

COOKING VEAL IN A GRILL PAN ACCENTUATES ITS DELICATE
FLAVOR AND FINE TEXTURE. WHEN CHOOSING VEAL CHOPS, THE
MEAT SHOULD BE PALE AND CREAMY WITH A LITTLE GRAY-
ISH PINK, AND THE SMALL AMOUNT OF FAT SHOULD BE WHITE.
VEAL AND ARTICHOKES ARE A TRADITIONAL MARRIAGE IN
ITALIAN CUISINE; I LIKE TO LEAVE THE FORK AND KNIFE ON
THE TABLE AND SAVOR THIS DISH WITH MY HANDS.

Veal Chops with
Baby Artichokes and Shallots

SERVES 2 AS A MAIN COURSE

2 veal rib chops (6 to 8 ounces each),
$^3/_4$ inch thick

4 sprigs fresh tarragon,
leaves removed from stems

1 clove garlic, finely minced or
crushed with a garlic press

$^1/_2$ teaspoon salt

$^1/_4$ teaspoon freshly ground pepper

4 baby artichokes

$^1/_2$ lemon

4 shallots, peeled and halved

2 tablespoons light olive oil

Trim any excess fat from the edges of the chops. Finely chop half the tarragon leaves and combine with the garlic, salt, and pepper. Rub the seasoning mixture into both sides of the chops. Let stand, covered, at room temperature for 10 to 20 minutes.

Prepare the artichokes as described on page 15. Set the artichokes, stem side down, in a steamer basket within a pan containing at least 1 inch of boiling water. Cover and steam until the bases are tender, about 15 minutes. Cool slightly and, when cool enough to handle, gently cut them in half lengthwise. Assemble the artichokes and shallots cut side up on a platter or cutting board. Brush the cut sides with olive oil and season with salt and pepper.

Preheat a grill pan over medium heat until very hot. Place the chops in the center of the pan and place the artichokes and shallots cut side down around the edges (allow the chops plenty of room so they sear nicely). Brush the tops of the artichokes and shallots with a little more olive oil and season with a little more salt and pepper. Cook for 3 to 4 minutes, then turn the chops, artichokes, and shallots over. Cook for an additional 3 minutes, or until the centers of the chops spring back when pressed with a fingertip. Serve immediately.

THE PORTERHOUSE STEAK IS A FAVORITE OF SO MANY PEOPLE BECAUSE IT HAS TWO CUTS OF BEEF IN ONE STEAK. IT CONTAINS A SOFT AND RICH TENDERLOIN AS WELL AS FIRM-TEXTURED JUICY SIRLOIN STRIP SEPARATED BY THE T-SHAPED BONE. THE GREEN PEPPERCORN SAUCE TAKES A FEW MINUTES TO PRE-PARE, BUT THE RESULT IS CLASSIC AND SURE TO IMPRESS, ESPECIALLY WHEN SERVED WITH PEARL ONIONS AND SWEET PEAS (PAGE 14). BE SURE TO USE THE GREEN PEPPER-CORNS PACKED IN BRINE, WHICH ARE AVAILABLE AT MOST SUPERMARKETS.

Cowboy Porterhouse Steak with Green Peppercorn Sauce

SERVES 2 AS A MAIN COURSE

1 porterhouse steak (about $1^1/_2$ pounds), $1^1/_4$ inches thick

Freshly ground pepper

Green Peppercorn Sauce (recipe follows)

Pat the steak dry with a paper towel. Season each side with pepper to taste and let stand at room temperature, covered, for 30 minutes.

Preheat a grill pan over medium heat until very hot. Place the steak in the pan and cook without moving until seared and nicely browned on one side, about 5 minutes. Turn the steak and cook 5 minutes more for medium rare, 6 minutes more for medium, or until the center of the steak springs back when pressed with a fingertip. Transfer the steak to a cutting board and let rest for 5 minutes. Cut the steak from the bone on both sides, then carve the steak into $1/_2$-inch-thick slices. Serve immediately on warm plates and spoon the Green Peppercorn Sauce on top.

Green Peppercorn Sauce

1 tablespoon light olive oil

1 tablespoon finely chopped shallot

1 garlic clove, finely chopped
or crushed with a garlic press

1 1/2 teaspoons brine-packed green
peppercorns, rinsed and drained

1 cup dry red wine such as
Cabernet Sauvignon

1 cup homemade or canned
chicken stock

1/2 cup water

2 tablespoons very cold unsalted
butter, cut in small pieces

1/4 teaspoon salt

1/4 teaspoon freshly ground pepper

In a medium saucepan, heat the oil over medium heat. Add the shallot and cook for about 2 minutes, stirring often, until golden. Add the garlic and half the green peppercorns and cook until you can smell the garlic, about 1 minute. Pour in the wine and bring to a boil. Cook until reduced to a syrupy consistency, about 10 minutes. Add the stock and water and continue cooking until the liquid is reduced to about 1 cup, 10 to 11 minutes. Strain the sauce into a small, clean saucepan.

Off the heat, whisk in the butter a little at a time, stirring constantly until the butter is absorbed. Stir in the remaining green peppercorns and season to taste with salt and pepper. Keep warm until ready for use. (The sauce can be made up to 1 day in advance, covered and refrigerated.) If the sauce cools, it must be reheated in a double boiler over hot but not simmering water, and whisked constantly. If the sauce gets too hot, the butter will separate out and rise to the top.

THE FILETS YOU CHOOSE FOR THIS DISH SHOULD BE
THE FINEST YOU CAN FIND. WHEN YOU TAKE THAT FIRST BITE,
EVERY INGREDIENT IN THIS SALAD WILL SING IN PERFECT
HARMONY. THE DRESSING FOR THIS RECIPE IS COMPRISED SOLELY
OF REDUCED BALSAMIC VINEGAR MADE IN ITALY BY MASTER-
FULLY AGING WHITE TREBBIANO GRAPE JUICE IN BARRELS UNTIL
DARK AND SWEET.

Baby Spinach and Steak Salad with Trebbiano Dressing

SERVES 2 AS A MAIN COURSE

$1/2$ cup balsamic vinegar

1 bunch (about 2 cups) baby spinach leaves, well washed and dried

$1/2$ medium red onion, halved and sliced in lengthwise strips

1 large portobello mushroom, gills and stem removed and cut into 1-inch cubes

2 teaspoons light olive oil

2 filets mignons, (6 ounces each), about $1/2$ inch thick, at room temperature

Salt and freshly ground pepper

2 hard-cooked eggs, whites and yolks chopped separately

1 large ear sweet white corn, kernels removed (about $1/2$ cup)

To make the dressing, cook the vinegar in a shallow, heavy pan at a low simmer for about 8 minutes, or until reduced by half. Transfer the dressing to a small glass or ceramic dish and let cool to room temperature. To drizzle, use a small spoon or place in a squeeze bottle.

Place the spinach in a large glass or non-reactive metal bowl and set aside. In a small bowl, toss the onion and mushroom with the olive oil.

Preheat a grill pan over medium heat until very hot. Add the mushroom and onion. Cook for 3 minutes, stirring until softened. Push the mushroom and onion to the side of the pan. Season both sides of the steaks with salt and pepper and place on the hot pan. Grill 4 minutes and turn. Grill an additional 4 minutes, or until to desired doneness. Transfer the steaks to a cutting board, cover loosely with foil, and let rest for 4 minutes.

Add the cooked mushroom mixture to the spinach and gently toss together. Divide the spinach mixture on two plates. Slice the steaks crosswise into $1/4$-inch strips and arrange on top of the spinach mixture. Sprinkle with the chopped egg and the corn kernels. Drizzle the reduced balsamic vinegar over the salads and serve immediately.

1 flank steak (about 1 pound)

1 green onion, white and 2 inches
of the green part, coarsely chopped

2 large jalapeño chiles, seeded
and coarsely chopped

YOU MAY SUBSTITUTE SKIRT STEAK FOR FLANK STEAK,
IF YOU CAN FIND IT. ANOTHER CUT FROM THE BEEF FLANK,
SKIRT STEAK IS MORE TRADITIONALLY USED IN REAL
SOUTHWESTERN FAJITAS. DON'T TRY TO COOK FLANK OR
SKIRT STEAK TO THE WELL-DONE STAGE OR IT WILL BE
AS TOUGH AS SHOE LEATHER!

Sizzlin' Fajitas

SERVES 4 AS A MAIN COURSE

1 cup loosely packed fresh
cilantro leaves

4 tablespoons light olive oil
or canola oil

2 tablespoons fresh lime juice

$1/4$ teaspoon salt

$1/4$ teaspoon freshly ground pepper

8 large flour tortillas

1 red bell pepper, cored, seeded,
and cut into $1/4$-inch strips

1 yellow bell pepper, cored, seeded,
and cut into $1/4$-inch strips

1 Anaheim chile, cored, seeded,
and cut into $1/4$-inch strips

1 small yellow onion, peeled, halved
lengthwise, and cut into thin strips

1 medium Haas avocado, pitted,
peeled, and cut into thin slices

1 cup good-quality bottled salsa

Place the steak in a glass or ceramic baking dish. In a food processor or blender, purée the green onion, jalapeño, cilantro, 3 tablespoons of the oil, lime juice, salt, and pepper. Pour the mixture over the steak and turn to coat both sides evenly. Cover and marinate at room temperature for 1 to 2 hours, turning at least once.

Wrap the tortillas in foil and warm in the oven at 150°F while you cook the steak and vegetables.

Preheat a grill pan over medium heat until very hot. Brush the peppers and onions with the remaining tablespoon of olive oil. Add the vegetables to the grill pan and cook, turning often with tongs until softened, about 4 minutes. Transfer to a glass or nonreactive metal bowl and cover to keep warm. Drain the marinade from the steak, place the steak in the hot grill pan, and grill for 4 minutes. Turn and cook until seared and nicely browned. Transfer the steak to a cutting board and cover loosely with foil. Let rest for 5 minutes, and then carve the meat across the grain into $1/4$-inch-thick slices. Cut these slices lengthwise in thirds and season with salt. Arrange the meat on a platter with the peppers and onions. Serve with the avocado, salsa, and the warmed tortillas, wrapping a few pieces of meat and some vegetables inside each one.

WHEN I CATERED ON MOVIE SETS THIS WAS A FAVORITE MIDDAY SNACK. I WOULD SPLIT BIG, SOFT HOAGIE ROLLS AND STUFF THEM FULL OF THE SAUSAGE AND PEPPER MIXTURE. THIS SNACK WAS ALWAYS WELCOME, UNTIL ONE DAY THE STAR OF THE FILM WAS DEVOURING ONE OF THESE MASSIVE CREATIONS AND JUICE DRIPPED ALL OVER HER COSTUME. THE ENTIRE SHOOT STOPPED UNTIL SHE WAS CLEANED UP. THE ONLY PERSON WHO WAS NOT HAPPY WAS THE DIRECTOR; EVERYONE ELSE CONTINUED TO FEAST ON MY AFTERNOON TREAT.

Italian Sausages and Sweet Peppers

SERVES 2 AS A SNACK OR LIGHT MAIN COURSE

1 pound fresh Italian sausage

1 red bell pepper, cored, seeded, and sliced lengthwise into $1/4$-inch strips

1 yellow bell pepper, cored, seeded, and sliced lengthwise into $1/4$-inch strips

1 poblano chile, stemmed, seeded, and sliced lengthwise into $1/4$-inch strips

$1/4$ cup light olive oil

$1/4$ teaspoon salt

$1/4$ teaspoon freshly ground pepper

Preheat a grill pan over medium heat until very hot. Pierce each of the sausages through at right angles with two wooden skewers that have been soaked in water for 15 minutes (this helps to hold their shape, and makes it easier to turn them). Brush all the pepper strips with olive oil and season them with salt and pepper. Place the sausages and peppers in the hot pan, making sure not to crowd them. Using tongs, turn the peppers often. Turn the sausages after about 6 minutes when they are nicely marked by the ridges of the pan. Continue cooking for another 6 minutes, until the peppers are tender and the sausages are crisp and firm. Remove from the pan; eat inside a sandwich, over pasta, or on its own with lemon wedges.

I PREFER THE "CHICAGO-CUT," OR THICK-CUT, PORK CHOPS FOR THE GRILL PAN BECAUSE THE THICKER CUT RETAINS ITS MOISTURE BETTER. MADE WITH NORMANDY APPLES IN NORTHERN FRANCE, CALVADOS HAS BECOME A VERY POPULAR BRANDY IN THE LAST FEW YEARS. IN FACT, THERE ARE MORE THAN 2,000 WEB SITES DEDICATED TO THE SPIRIT, COMPLETE WITH RECIPES AND OTHER USEFUL HINTS. TRY THIS DISH WITH NEW POTATOES WITH HICKORY-SMOKED WILD BOAR BACON (PAGE 34).

Chicago-Cut Pork Chops with Calvados Chutney

SERVES 2 AS A MAIN COURSE

2 Chicago-cut pork chops,
cut at least 1 inch thick

$1/4$ teaspoon salt

$1/4$ teaspoon freshly ground pepper

Calvados Chutney
(recipe follows)

Preheat a grill pan over medium heat until very hot. Season both sides of the chops with salt and pepper. Add to the pan and cook for 5 minutes. Turn and cook for 5 minutes more, or until the centers of the chops spring back when pressed with a fingertip. Transfer to warm plates and top with Calvados Chutney.

Calvados Chutney

1 1/2 cups Golden Delicious apples,
peeled, cored, and cubed

1 tablespoon fresh lemon juice

2 tablespoons unsalted butter,
at room temperature

1 teaspoon sugar

1/4 cup Calvados

1/4 cup apple cider

Toss the apples with the lemon juice as soon as they are cut. Preheat a small saucepan over medium heat until hot. Add the butter and the apples and cook for about 3 minutes, or until the apples begin to soften. Add the sugar, Calvados, and cider. Cook, stirring occasionally, until the mixture begins to thicken, about 5 minutes. Set the pan aside and loosely cover until ready to serve.

Chicago-Cut Pork Chops

with Calvados Chutney

THE RAINBOW OF BELL PEPPERS AVAILABLE TODAY ENABLES YOU
TO HAVE FUN WITH THIS DISH. EXPERIMENT WITH DIFFERENT
COMBINATIONS TO CREATE EXCITING COLORFUL KABOBS!

Beef Kabobs
with Asian Marinade

SERVES 2 AS A MAIN COURSE

MARINADE

2 tablespoons sesame oil

$1/_4$ cup low-sodium soy sauce

$1/_4$ cup rice vinegar

1 tablespoon crushed garlic

2 teaspoons grated fresh ginger

$1/_2$ teaspoon red pepper flakes

————

8 ounces boneless beef steak,
cut in 1-inch cubes

6 large button mushrooms,
wiped clean and quartered

$1/_2$ red bell pepper, cored, seeded,
and cut into 1-inch pieces

$1/_2$ yellow bell pepper, cored, seeded,
and cut into 1-inch pieces

Wooden skewers, soaked in water
for 15 minutes

To make the marinade:

In a baking dish stir together the sesame
oil, soy sauce, vinegar, garlic, ginger,
and pepper flakes.

Add the beef, mushrooms, and bell peppers to the marinade, and turn to coat all
the ingredients evenly. Cover and let stand
at room temperature for at least 1 hour,
or in the refrigerator for up to 4 hours.
Thread each skewer, alternating pieces of
beef, mushrooms, and bell peppers.

Preheat a grill pan over medium heat until
very hot. Cook the skewers for 4 minutes,
turn and cook 4 minutes more. Serve
immediately.

POULTRY

I have discovered that the optimal cooking technique for poultry is using a grill pan. Without using any oil, a boneless, skinless breast of chicken is plump, juicy, and flavorful within minutes. The recipes in this chapter include classics such as Grilled Chicken Caesar Salad and Chicken Saté, as well as more exotic flavors like those of Rock Cornish Game Hens with Mango Salsa and Smoked Duck Sausage with Red Pear Sauce. Poultry is the blank canvas of the kitchen. With the grill pan the possibilities become endless.

THIS RECIPE SHOULD DO TWO THINGS: TEACH YOU HOW DELICIOUS A CHICKEN BREAST CAN BE IN THE GRILL PAN, AND SHARE WITH YOU MY LOVE FOR THOSE LITTLE GREEN GEMS KNOWN AS TOMATILLOS. THE TOMATILLOS ARE SUCH A PLEASANT SURPRISE IN THIS TART SALSA. THE COMBINATION OF THE WARM GRILLED CHICKEN AND THIS FRESH, MODERN-DAY CONDIMENT IS CERTAINLY A MOUTHFUL!

Chicken Breasts with Tomatillo Salsa

SERVES 2 AS A MAIN COURSE

2 boneless, skinless chicken breast halves, washed and patted dry

Salt and freshly ground pepper

Tomatillo Salsa
(recipe follows)

Preheat a grill pan over medium heat until very hot. Season both sides of the chicken with salt and pepper to taste. Grill the chicken for about 4 minutes on each side, until firm. Transfer to warm plates and spoon the salsa over the chicken. Serve immediately.

Tomatillo Salsa

8 medium tomatillos, husked, rinsed, and coarsely chopped (about 1 $^1/_2$ cups)

$^1/_4$ cup finely diced red onion

2 tablespoons finely diced jalapeño chile

2 tablespoons fresh lime juice

1 $^1/_2$ tablespoons light olive oil

2 tablespoons coarsely chopped cilantro

$^1/_4$ teaspoon salt

$^1/_4$ teaspoon freshly ground pepper

In a glass or nonreactive metal bowl, combine the tomatillos, onion, chile, lime juice, olive oil, cilantro, salt, and pepper. Cover and set aside, or refrigerate for up to 2 hours.

THE CURRENT AVAILABILITY OF UNUSUAL MEATS AND GAME HAS LENT NEW CREATIVITY TO MY MENUS. NOT ONE TO STICK WITH STANDARD FARE, I AM CONSTANTLY SEARCHING OUT SOURCES FOR FRESH AND UNUSUAL PRODUCTS TO TRY.

THIS DISH IS UNFORGETTABLE SERVED AS AN APPETIZER— BUT MAKE PLENTY, THIS IS A FAVORITE. I USE RED PEARS FOR THE SAUCE, BUT BOSC PEARS OR EVEN APPLES MAY BE SUBSTITUTED.

Smoked Duck Sausage with Red Pear Sauce

SERVES 2 AS AN APPETIZER

DIPPING SAUCE

4 ripe red pears, peeled, cored, and cut into chunks

1 tablespoon fresh lemon juice

$1/4$ teaspoon ground cloves

———

$1/2$ pound duck sausage, cut into 1-inch pieces

Small decorative skewers or toothpicks

To make the dipping sauce:

Place the pears, lemon juice, and cloves in a food processor or blender, and process until smooth. Transfer to a small glass or nonreactive metal bowl. (The sauce can be made up to 2 hours in advance and kept, tightly covered, in the refrigerator. Bring to room temperature before serving.)

Preheat a grill pan over medium heat until very hot. Place the sausage in the pan and cook, turning the pieces frequently with tongs. Continue cooking until firm, 7 to 10 minutes. Skewer the pieces of sausage individually and serve with the dipping sauce.

OCCASIONALLY WHEN I AM MAKING ANOTHER RECIPE
CALLING FOR CHICKEN BREAST, I MAKE TWO EXTRA BREASTS AND
STORE THEM IN THE REFRIGERATOR FOR THIS RECIPE.
THE CAESAR DRESSING IS SWEETENED WITH ROASTED GARLIC,
ADDING A NEW TWIST TO A CLASSIC DISH.

Grilled Chicken Caesar Salad

SERVES 2 AS A MAIN COURSE

CAESAR DRESSING

- 3 tablespoons fresh lemon juice
- 2 cloves Roasted Garlic (page 29)
- 1 teaspoon Dijon-style mustard
- 6 oil-packed flat anchovy fillets, drained and coarsely chopped
- $1/3$ cup light olive oil

_____

- 2 boneless, skinless chicken breast halves (5 to 6 ounces each), rinsed and patted dry
- $1/4$ teaspoon salt
- $1/4$ teaspoon freshly ground pepper
- $1/2$ head romaine lettuce, washed and dried
- $1/3$ cup freshly grated Parmesan cheese

To make the Caesar dressing:

In a food processor or blender, combine the lemon juice, garlic, mustard, and anchovies. Purée until smooth. With the motor running, gradually add the olive oil and blend until smooth.

Preheat a grill pan over medium heat until very hot. Season both sides of the chicken with salt and pepper. Add to the pan and cook for 5 minutes. Turn and cook for 5 minutes more, or until the center of the chicken springs back when pressed with a fingertip.

Transfer the chicken to a cutting board and slice into strips crosswise. Tear the lettuce into large pieces and place in a large glass or nonreactive metal bowl. Toss lightly with the dressing, then add the Parmesan and chicken and toss again gently. Serve immediately.

_____

I ENJOY SERVING THIS DISTINCTIVE DISH WITH WARM TORTILLAS.
THIS SALSA IS ALSO TERRIFIC SERVED WITH CHICKEN AND
FISH, AND THE SWEETNESS OF THE FRUIT MAKES IT A PERFECT
BREAKFAST TREAT ON BAGELS WITH CREAM CHEESE.

Rock Cornish Game Hens with Mango Salsa

SERVES 2 AS A MAIN COURSE

MANGO SALSA

2 large mangos, peeled, seeded, and coarsely chopped

$1/4$ cup finely sliced red onion

$1/4$ cup finely sliced red bell pepper

1 tablespoon minced jalapeño chiles

$1/4$ cup fresh lime juice

$1/4$ cup coarsely chopped cilantro

$1/4$ teaspoon salt

$1/4$ teaspoon freshly ground pepper

———

2 Rock Cornish game hens ($1 1/2$ to 2 pounds each), halved lengthwise, well rinsed and patted dry

Salt and freshly ground pepper

To make the mango salsa:

In a medium glass or nonreactive metal bowl, combine the mango, red onion, bell pepper, chiles, lime juice, cilantro, salt, and pepper. Cover and refrigerate for at least 1 hour and no more than 3 hours. Bring to room temperature before serving.

Preheat a grill pan over medium heat until very hot. Season both sides of the hens with additional salt and pepper. Place the hens in the grill pan, breast side down, and cook for 10 minutes. Turn and cook for 10 minutes more. Transfer the hens to warm plates and serve with the Mango Salsa.

———

I HAVE BEEN MAKING THIS RELISH FOR YEARS AS AN UNUSUAL
THANKSGIVING CONDIMENT. I ALWAYS BUY AS MANY BAGS
OF CRANBERRIES AS I CAN WHEN THEY APPEAR IN THE MARKET
AND FREEZE THEM SO I CAN ENJOY THIS THROUGHOUT
THE YEAR. IF YOU ARE FAMILIAR WITH THE TECHNIQUE, TRY
CANNING THIS ZESTY RELISH.

Turkey Breast with Cranberry-Tangerine Relish

SERVES 2 AS A MAIN COURSE

CRANBERRY-TANGERINE RELISH

$1/2$ cup (1 stick) unsalted butter

2 cups fresh cranberries, rinsed and picked over

$1/2$ cup sugar

1 cup fresh orange juice

2 cups canned mandarin oranges, drained

$1/4$ cup coarsely chopped fresh mint leaves, plus 2 extra sprigs for garnish

———

2 boneless, skinless turkey cutlets, 5 to 6 ounces each, rinsed and patted dry

$1/4$ teaspoon salt

$1/4$ teaspoon freshly ground pepper

To make the cranberry-tangerine relish:

In a medium skillet, melt the butter over medium heat. Add the cranberries and sauté for about 4 minutes, until they begin to burst. Add the sugar and sauté for 2 minutes more. Add the orange juice and let simmer for about 6 minutes, until the mixture begins to thicken. Remove from the heat and let cool to room temperature. Transfer to a medium glass or nonreactive metal bowl and gently stir in the oranges and mint. Let stand, loosely covered, for at least 1 hour at room temperature. (The relish can be made 1 day in advance and kept in the refrigerator. Bring to room temperature before serving.)

Preheat a grill pan over medium heat until very hot. Season the turkey with salt and pepper, add to the pan, and cook for 5 minutes. Turn and cook for 5 minutes more, until the center of the turkey springs back when pressed with a fingertip. Transfer to warm plates, top with the relish, and garnish with a sprig of mint.

A HAMBURGER WITHOUT GUILT! YOU CAN SUBSTITUTE GROUND
CHICKEN FOR THIS RECIPE IF YOU WISH. I SERVE THIS
WITH PLENTY OF BAKED POTATO CHIPS IN KEEPING WITH THE
LEAN THEME OF THIS DISH.

Turkey Burgers with Gruyère Cheese on Sourdough Bread

SERVES 2 AS A MAIN COURSE

$1/2$ pound ground turkey

$1/4$ teaspoon salt

$1/4$ teaspoon freshly ground pepper

$1/4$ cup sliced cremini mushrooms

$1/2$ cup shredded Gruyère cheese

4 thick slices of sourdough bread, toasted

Preheat a grill pan over medium heat until very hot. Divide the ground turkey in half and gently shape it into two burgers, handling it as little as possible. Season the two burgers with salt and pepper. Add the burgers and the sliced mushrooms to the pan and cook for 5 minutes. Turn the burgers and cook for 5 minutes more, then top with cheese. Remove from the heat and let the burgers sit in the pan for 2 minutes, or until the cheese melts. Place the burgers on the toasted bread and spoon the mushrooms on top. Serve immediately.

THE PEANUT SAUCE IS ALWAYS EVERYONE'S FAVORITE PART OF
THIS DISH. MAKE ENOUGH TO PLACE A LITTLE DISH ON
EACH PLATE, ENABLING YOUR DINING COMPANIONS TO "DOUBLE
DIP" THEIR CHICKEN.

Chicken Saté with Peanut Sauce

SERVES 2 AS A MAIN COURSE OR 4 AS AN APPETIZER

PEANUT SAUCE

1 cup unsalted, roasted peanuts

1/4 cup low-sodium soy sauce

1/4 cup honey

1/3 cup plum wine
(available in Asian markets)

2 small dried red chiles,
stemmed and seeded

1/2 cup sesame oil

————

2 boneless, skinless chicken breast
halves, 5 to 6 ounces each, well
rinsed, patted dry, and sliced
into 1/4-inch strips

10 wooden skewers, soaked in water
for 15 minutes

1/4 teaspoon salt

1/4 teaspoon freshly ground pepper

To make the peanut sauce:

Put the peanuts in a food processor or blender, and process until finely ground. With the motor running, add the soy sauce, honey, plum wine, chiles, and oil. Continue to process until smooth. Transfer to a glass or nonreactive metal bowl, cover, and refrigerate until ready to use. (The sauce can be made 3 days in advance. Bring to room temperature before using.)

Skewer each strip of the chicken lengthwise and season to taste with salt and pepper.

Preheat a grill pan over medium heat until very hot. Cook the chicken for 3 minutes, then turn and cook for 3 minutes more. Transfer to warm plates and serve with the peanut sauce on the side for dipping.

————

IN THIS DISH, THE OIL FROM THE ROASTED GARLIC WILL
DRIP ONTO THE CHICKEN, MARINATING IT. TO ADD ADDITIONAL
FLAVOR, MARINATE THE CHICKEN IN LEMON-HERB BASTING
SAUCE (PAGE 28).

Garlic Chicken Kabobs on Rosemary Skewers

SERVES 2 AS A MAIN COURSE

10 long, sturdy sprigs
of fresh rosemary

1 pound boneless, skinless chicken
breasts, cut into 1-inch cubes

10 cloves Roasted Garlic (page 29)

$^1/_2$ teaspoon salt

$^1/_4$ teaspoon freshly ground pepper

1 lemon, sliced $^1/_4$ inch thick

Leaving a bushy "top," strip the needle-shaped leaves from the bottom $^7/_8$ of each rosemary sprig to make a "skewer." Thread the chicken cubes on the skewers, placing 1 roasted garlic clove between each two cubes. Season the skewers with salt and pepper to taste.

Preheat a grill pan over medium heat until very hot. Add the chicken kabobs and scatter the sliced lemon around the pan. Grill for 4 minutes on each side, until the chicken is firm. Sprinkle with additional salt and pepper. Serve immediately.

See page 28 for Vegetable Kabobs with Lemon-Herb Basting Sauce.

Spicy and sweet, these little delicacies are best served on a platter and eaten with your hands. If you are serving them as party hors d'oeuvres, make plenty of them and have the napkins close by.

Chicken Wings with Chiles and Lime

SERVES 2 AS AN APPETIZER

$^1/_2$ cup fresh lime juice

4 cloves garlic, crushed

4 teaspoons grated fresh ginger

3 jalapeño chiles, seeded and finely chopped

2 dried red chiles, seeded and finely chopped

2 pounds chicken wings and drummettes

Combine the lime juice, garlic, ginger, and chiles in a glass or nonreactive metal bowl. Add the chicken and turn to coat evenly. Cover and refrigerate for at least 1 hour and up to 4 hours, turning occasionally. Remove from the refrigerator and let stand at room temperature for 20 minutes.

Preheat a grill pan over medium heat until very hot. Add the chicken and grill for about 20 minutes, turning occasionally, until cooked through and firm. Serve immediately.

THIS RECIPE MAKES A CLASSIC PESTO, SIMILAR TO WHAT YOU
MIGHT FIND ON A MENU IN A CALIFORNIA-ITALIAN
"TRATTORIA," EXCEPT I MAKE MINE WITH ROASTED GARLIC.
YOU CAN EXPERIMENT AND SUBSTITUTE DIFFERENT HERBS FOR
THE BASIL AND PARSLEY, SUCH AS CILANTRO OR MINT.

Pesto Chicken with Fettuccine

SERVES 2 AS A MAIN COURSE

PESTO

$^1/_2$ cup fresh parsley leaves

1 cup fresh basil leaves

3 cloves Roasted Garlic (page 29)

1 tablespoon pine nuts

$^1/_3$ cup light olive oil

———

2 boneless, skinless chicken breast
halves, rinsed and patted dry

$^1/_2$ tablespoon salt

$^1/_4$ teaspoon freshly ground pepper

$^1/_4$ pound dried fettuccine

To make the pesto:

Combine the parsley, basil, garlic, and
pine nuts in a food processor or blender.
Process until a paste forms. With the
motor running, add the olive oil slowly,
and continue processing until well
blended.

Preheat a grill pan over medium heat until
very hot. Season both sides of the
chicken breasts with half of the salt and
all of the pepper. Add the chicken to the
pan and cook for 4 minutes. Turn and
cook for 4 minutes more, or until the center of the chicken springs back when
pressed with a fingertip. While the chicken
is cooking, bring a large pot of water to

boil. Add the remaining salt and the
fettuccine. Cook at a rolling boil until the
pasta is just tender, about 7 minutes.
Drain the pasta well and toss with half
of the pesto. Transfer the chicken to a cutting board, spread the remaining pesto
on both sides, and cut into crosswise
strips. Place equal portions of the pasta on
warm plates. Drape the chicken over the
pasta and serve.

PURVEYORS AND MAIL-ORDER SOURCES

Several grill pans are available
in stores today. I have used all of the
ones listed and have found that
they each have a significant value.
Square versus round—for the
sake of balance, if you have round
burners, use a round grill pan, a
square pan for square burners.
The most common interior finishes
on grill pans are non-stick, stick
resistant, enamel, and cast iron. All
grill pans must be preheated over
medium heat until very hot before
placing any food in them, and unless
you are seasoning a cast-iron pan,
do not spray or pour oil into the
grill pan.

Cookware

All-Clad Metalcrafters, Inc.
424 Morganza Road
Canonsburg, PA 15317
(412) 745-8300
ANODIZED ALUMINUM WITH A
NON-STICK FINISH

Calphalon Corporation
P.O. Box 583
Toledo, OH 43697
(800) 809-7267
ANODIZED ALUMINUM, AVAILABLE WITH
A NON-STICK OR STICK-RESISTANT FINISH

Le Creuset of America
1 Bob Gifford Boulevard
Early Branch, SC 29916
(803) 943-4308
ENAMEL-FINISHED CAST IRON WITH
A STICK-RESISTANT INTERIOR, AVAILABLE
IN SEVERAL COLORS

Lodge Manufacturing Company
P.O. Box 380
South Pittsburg, TN 37380
(615) 837-7181
A ONE-HUNDRED-YEAR-OLD, FAMILY-OWNED
FOUNDRY, PRODUCING ORIGINAL AMERICAN
CAST-IRON COOKWARE

Specialty Gourmet Foods

Bittersweet Herb Farm
P.O. Box 679
Charlemont, MA 01339
(800) 456-1599
FLAVORED BALSAMIC VINEGARS AND OILS

Frieda's, Inc.
P.O. Box 58488
Los Angeles, CA 90058
(800) 241-1771
SPECIALTY PRODUCE SUPPLIERS AVAILABLE
AT MOST GOURMET SUPERMARKETS

House of Smoke, Inc.
825 Denver Avenue
Fort Lupton, CO 80621
(800) 738-2750
THE FINEST PURVEYOR OF WILD GAME
AND EXOTIC MEATS I HAVE EVER FOUND.
THE AVAILABILITY OF CERTAIN ITEMS
CHANGES MONTHLY, SO CALL FOR
A PRODUCT LIST.

Morton & Bassett Spices
32 Pamaron Way
Novato, CA 94949
(415) 883-8530
A FULL LINE OF THE HIGHEST-QUALITY
SPICES AND HERBS, AVAILABLE AT MOST
SUPERMARKETS NATIONWIDE

Several purveyors of fine products have contributed to my growing pantry. I encourage you to experiment with some of these delicacies. They may inspire you.

Index

TABLE OF EQUIVALENTS

The exact equivalents in the tables at right have been rounded for convenience.

Liquid Measures

U.S.		METRIC
$\frac{1}{4}$	TEASPOON	1.25 MILLILITERS
$\frac{1}{2}$	TEASPOON	2.5 MILLILITERS
1	TEASPOON	5 MILLILITERS
1	TABLESPOON (3 TEASPOONS)	15 MILLILITERS
1	FLUID OUNCE (2 TABLESPOONS)	30 MILLILITERS
$\frac{1}{4}$	CUP	60 MILLILITERS
$\frac{1}{3}$	CUP	80 MILLILITERS
$\frac{1}{2}$	CUP	120 MILLILITERS
1	CUP	240 MILLILITERS
1	PINT (2 CUPS)	480 MILLILITERS
1	QUART (4 CUPS, 32 OUNCES)	960 MILLILITERS
1	GALLON (4 QUARTS)	3.84 LITERS

Dry Measures

U.S.		METRIC
1	OUNCE (BY WEIGHT)	28 GRAMS
1	POUND	454 GRAMS
2.2	POUNDS	1 KILOGRAM

Length

U.S.		METRIC
$\frac{1}{8}$	INCH	3 MILLIMETERS
$\frac{1}{4}$	INCH	6 MILLIMETERS
$\frac{1}{2}$	INCH	12 MILLIMETERS
1	INCH	2.5 CENTIMETERS

Oven Temperature

FAHRENHEIT	CELSIUS	GAS
250	120	$\frac{1}{2}$
275	140	1
300	150	2
325	160	3
350	180	4
375	190	5
400	200	6
425	220	7
450	230	8
475	240	9
500	260	10